My Favorite Quotations

My Favorite Quotations

Norman Vincent Peale

A Giniger Book
published in association with

HarperSanFrancisco
A Division of HarperCollins*Publishers*

MY FAVORITE QUOTATIONS. Copyright © 1990 by Norman Vincent Peale. All rights reserved. Published in association with The K. S. Giniger Company, Inc., 250 West 57th Street, New York, NY 10107. Printed in the United States of America. No part of this book may be used or reproduced in any manner whatsoever without written permission except in the case of brief quotations embodied in critical articles and reviews. For information address HarperCollins Publishers, 10 East 53rd Street, New York, NY 10022.

INTERIOR DESIGN BY RICK CHAFIAN

Library of Congress Cataloging-in-Publication Data

Peale, Norman Vincent, 1898–
   My favorite quotations / Norman Vincent Peale — 1st ed.
     p. cm.
   "A Giniger book."
   ISBN 0-06-066483-5
   1. Conduct of life — Quotations, maxims, etc. I. Title.
PN6084. C556P42   1990
082 — dc20   89-45895
                                                      CIP

91 92 93 94 K.P. 10 9 8 7 6 5

This edition is printed on acid-free paper that meets the American National Standards Institute Z39.48 Standard.

Contents

Acknowledgments

I appreciate the efficient work on this manuscript of my secretaries Sybil Light and Nancy Dakin and the research of Donald T. Kauffman.

Introduction

Winston Churchill once said, "It is a good thing to read books of quotations. The quotations when engraved upon the memory give you good thoughts."

And to have "good thoughts" is important, for a person becomes what he thinks. Gautama Buddha told us that. "Mind is everything," he said. "We become what we think."

Charles Edison, one-time governor of New Jersey and son of the famous inventor Thomas A. Edison, was a personal friend of mine; I was with him many times. He loved to talk about his father and told me many stories about him.

It seems that the older Edison thought that the mind is our greatest asset and would often say to his son, "The primary function of the body is to carry the brain." That is not a direct quotation, being simply a remark in conversation, but it may be taken to represent the inventor's thinking. The brain, besides directing motor activity, is, of course, the instrument by which one remembers, considers, evaluates, thinks. And it is through the wonders of the brain that one knows God, the Creator of it all.

William James, sometimes called the father of American psychological science, expressed agreement with these ideas and went even further: "The greatest discovery of my generation is that human beings can alter their lives by altering their attitudes of mind." Professor James's generation lived in what may be called an age of discovery. During that era some of the most notable discoveries of science took place. But the supreme discovery is that we can change our lives by the changing of mental attitudes.

That being true—and that it is true is a generally accepted fact today—then anything that can contribute to a thought process that changes our basic attitudes is of value. I have found over many years that the habit of dropping choice thoughts into consciousness and allowing them to permeate the mental structure results finally in a thought pattern that affects virtually the totality of one's life.

The quotation just cited from William James, for example, was dropped into my thoughts one day long ago as I sat in class at Boston University. It was as if I had been hit by a bolt of lightning. It struck me so forcibly that it vitally affected my total thinking. The truth of it seemed certain. I believed it; I accepted it. From my background, I associated personal change with faith and, in a flash of insight, knew that I could change my life by changing my attitudes of mind. I've been advocating that truth about people ever since.

So the object of this book of quotations is to bring to readers the thoughts I have picked up in a lifetime of reading, as well as others heard in conversation with all sorts of people. All wisdom is not in the past. But, when working with quotations, an old saying often comes to mind: "There is nothing new under the sun." Often today's speakers, writers, and conversationalists may come up with a new formulation of an ancient truth that is fascinating, even exciting. We may expect that these truths may continue to be quoted 100 years from now, perhaps modernized to fit the late twenty-first century.

I have had a lot of pleasure in gathering together these favorite quotations. Incidents in which the quotations have been meaningful to me have come to mind as I collected them for this book. I could actually make another book of stories about those incidents. But for now, just read a few of these quotations at a time and let them "germinate," shall we say, in your consciousness. They may start something. And, when engraved upon the memory, as Churchill said, they will indeed "give you good thoughts."

I hope that you have as much pleasure in reading them as I did when putting them together in this book. And may I add perhaps the greatest quotation of all, though I do not know who first said it: "God bless you."

Norman Vincent Peale

My Favorite Quotations

One
Daily Life and Work

———————◼———————

As I write this, autumn has returned to the Northeast where I live, and the hills and valleys are bathed in the special light that gives the landscape a crystal clarity.

Vacations are over, and most of us are busy with our work. For some, unfortunately, the daily routine is drudgery; the surveys say that millions of people hate their jobs. But it need not be so! For decades, I have been saying that an enthusiastic, positive outlook can transform any situation, and thousands of individuals testify to the truth of that claim.

It used to be stated—perhaps sometimes with justification—that religion was a matter of "pie in the sky by and by." But real religion is and always has been redemption in the here-and-now as well as a strongly based hope for the hereafter. The realities of faith, hope, and love can make every day an exciting adventure.

I contend that how you do something and the attitude with which you do it are usually even more important than what you do. The other day a friend remarked, "I just had a good, long walk to the post office, and I made an important discovery." When I asked him what he discovered, he said, "During the fall and winter, I try to get as much sun as possible. On my walk today, I could have been in the shade most of the time, but I found it was just as easy to walk on the sunny side of the street."

Often we have no choice about doing things, but we can always choose how to do them. And that, as the following quotations illustrate, can make all the difference in your daily life.

*Wherefore have ye not fulfilled your task?

EXODUS 5:14

■

The men did the work faithfully.

2 CHRONICLES 34:12

■

Establish thou the work of our hands upon us.

PSALM 90:17

*All of the quotations in each chapter appear in approximate chronological order by the birthdate of the authors. Anonymous quotations are placed in their estimated chronology.

Whatsoever thy hand findeth to do, do it with thy might.

ECCLESIASTES 9:10

He who labors diligently need never despair; for all things are accomplished by diligence and labor.

MENANDER (343–291 B.C.)

The life given us by nature is short, but the memory of a well-spent life is eternal.

MARCUS TULLIUS CICERO (106–43 B.C.)

In adversity remember to keep an even mind.

HORACE (QUINTUS HORATIUS FLACEUS, 65–8 B.C.)

A rolling stone gathers no moss.

PUBLILIUS SYRUS (ca. 42 B.C.)

It is a rough road that leads to the heights of greatness.

LUCIUS ANNAEUS SENECA (4 B.C.–A.D. 65)

Those who aim at great deeds must also suffer greatly.

PLUTARCH (46–120)

Not slothful in business; fervent in spirit; serving the Lord.

ROMANS 12:11

Vex not thy spirit at the course of things; they heed not thy vexation. How ludicrous and outlandish is astonishment at anything that may happen in life.

MARCUS AURELIUS (121–180)

Art is right reason in the doing of work.

ST. THOMAS AQUINAS (1225–1274)

Diligence is the mother of good luck, and God gives all things to industry.

BENJAMIN FRANKLIN (1706–1790)

One today is worth two tomorrows; never leave that till tomorrow which you can do today.

BENJAMIN FRANKLIN (1706–1790)

Never despair, but if you do, work on in despair.

EDMUND BURKE (1729–1797)

If at first you don't succeed, try, try again.

WILLIAM EDWARD HICKSON (1803–1870)

The world's a nettle; disturb it, it stings. Grasp it
firmly, it stings not.

EDWARD G. L. BULWER-LYTTON (1803–1873)

The heights by great men reached and kept
Were not attained by sudden flight,
But they, while their companions slept,
Were toiling upward in the night.

HENRY WADSWORTH LONGFELLOW (1807–1882)

Still achieving, still pursuing, learn to labor and to
wait.

HENRY WADSWORTH LONGFELLOW (1807–1882)

Men are born to succeed, not to fail.

HENRY DAVID THOREAU (1817–1862)

The greatest use of life is to spend it for something
that will outlast it.

WILLIAM JAMES (1842–1910)

Opportunity is missed by most people because it is
dressed in overalls and looks like work.

THOMAS A. EDISON (1847–1931)

In all human affairs there are *efforts,* and there are
results, and the strength of the effort is the measure
of the result.

JAMES ALLEN (1849–1925)

Turn your stumbling blocks into stepping stones.

ANONYMOUS

Strong people are made by opposition like kites that
go up against the wind.

FRANK HARRIS (1856–1931)

Always take an emergency leisurely.

CHINESE PROVERB

Be strong!
We are not here to play, to dream, to drift;
We have hard work to do and loads to lift;
Shun not the struggle—face it; 'tis God's gift.

MALTBIE D. BABCOCK (1858–1901)

We are so outnumbered there's only one thing to do.
We must attack.

SIR ANDREW CUNNINGHAM (1866–1963)

Choose your rut carefully; you'll be in it for the next
ten miles.

ROAD SIGN IN UPSTATE NEW YORK

In our day, when a pitcher got into trouble in a
game, instead of taking him out, our manager would
leave him in and tell him to pitch his way out of
trouble.

CY (DENTON TRUE) YOUNG (1867–1955)

It is a funny thing about life; if you refuse to accept
anything but the best, you very often get it.

W. SOMERSET MAUGHAM (1874–1965)

I have nothing to offer but blood, toil, tears, and
sweat.

WINSTON CHURCHILL (1874–1965)

It's the plugging away that will win you the day
So don't be a piker old pard!
Just draw on your grit; it's so easy to quit.
It's the keeping your chin up that's hard.

ROBERT W. SERVICE (1874–1958)

Truth has no special time of its own. Its hour is
now-always.

ALBERT SCHWEITZER (1875–1965)

I would never have amounted to anything were it not
for adversity. I was forced to come up the hard way.

J.C. PENNEY (1875–1971)

Problems are only opportunities in work clothes.

HENRY J. KAISER (1882–1967)

Grant me the courage not to give up even though I
think it is hopeless.

CHESTER W. NIMITZ (1885–1966)

Manual labor to my father was not only good and decent for its own sake, but as he was given to saying, it straightened out one's thoughts.

MARY ELLEN CHASE (1887–1973)

When the rock is hard, we get harder than the rock. When the job is tough, we get tougher than the job.

GEORGE CULLUM, SR. (1895–1983)

There is no sense in the struggle, but there is no choice but to struggle.

ERNIE PYLE (1900–1945)

To every disadvantage there is a corresponding advantage.

W. CLEMENT STONE (1902–   )

We have a problem. "Congratulations." But it's a tough problem. "Then double congratulations."

W. CLEMENT STONE (1902–   )

Strong lives are motivated by dynamic purposes.

KENNETH HILDEBRAND (1906–1979)

When the going gets tough, let the tough get going.

FRANK LEAHY (1908–1973)

I make steel for people but you put steel into people.

STEEL-COMPANY PRESIDENT

Work! Thank God for the swing of it, for the
clamoring, hammering ring of it.

ANGELA MORGAN (?–1957)

Two
Enthusiasm and Perseverance

Somewhere out of the past comes a story about three men helping build a cathedral. A passerby, watching one man digging at a wall for the foundation, asked him what he was doing. Between shovels full of earth he grunted, "I'm digging a hole."

A stonemason, asked the same question, answered, "Can't you see I'm making a wall?"

Another laborer was pushing a cart loaded with stones toward the construction site. When he was asked the question, his face lighted up with enthusiasm. He replied, "I'm building a cathedral."

Success at anything requires two vital ingredients: enthusiasm and perseverance. Both can be helped by the broad view that looks beyond temporary difficulties and disappointments to a great goal. What are you doing with your life? Are you putting in time or building something lasting and worthwhile? These are questions we must ask ourselves.

Enthusiasm is the priceless quality that makes everything different. The men and women who achieve the most are invariably inspired by enthusiasm. They approach life, its opportunities, and its problems with this vital characteristic.

Successful individuals also keep at it. Great ideas come to naught unless they are carried to completion. When Glenn Cunningham was seven years old, he was so badly burned in a schoolhouse fire that his doctor said, "I doubt if he'll be able to walk again." But the little boy had been motivated by his father to become a champion runner. He visualized himself winning races. Despite intense pain, he struggled to walk again, then to run, although all he could manage at first was a queer hippety-hop gait. But he kept running until he became the outstanding miler of his time.

As you cultivate enthusiasm and perseverance, more power to you!

He did it with all his heart, and prospered.

2 CHRONICLES 31:21

The people had a mind to work.

NEHEMIAH 4:6

Here am I; send me.

ISAIAH 6:8

A journey of 1,000 miles begins with a single step.

LAO-TZU (FIFTH CENTURY B.C.)

Do not count your chickens before they hatch.

AESOP (620–560 B.C.)

It takes a wise man to recognize a wise man.

XENOPHANES (570–480 B.C.)

When you have faults, do not fear to abandon them.

CONFUCIUS (551–479 B.C.)

God loves to help him who strives to help himself.

AESCHYLUS (525–456 B.C.)

Well begun is half done.

ARISTOTLE (384–322 B.C.)

The great man is he who does not lose his child's heart.

MENCIUS (371–288 B.C.)

Even God lends a hand to honest boldness.

MENANDER (343–291 B.C.)

The drops of rain make a hole in the stone not by violence but by oft falling.

LUCRETIUS (TITUS LUCRETIUS CARUS, 96–55 B.C.)

Let us go singing as far as we go; the road will be less tedious.

VIRGIL (PUBLIUS VERGILIUS MARO, 70–19 B.C.)

Better late than never.

LIVY (59 B.C.–A.D. 17)

Having done all, to stand.

EPHESIANS 6:13

This one thing I do, forgetting those things which are
behind, and reaching forth unto those things which
are before.

PHILIPPIANS 3:13

And whatsoever ye do, do it heartily.

COLOSSIANS 3:23

God helps those who persevere.

THE KORAN

Time is the most valuable thing a man can spend.

LAERTIUS DIOGENES (THIRD CENTURY)

The hammer shatters glass but forges steel.

RUSSIAN PROVERB

Trifles make perfection, but perfection is no trifle.

MICHELANGELO (1475–1564)

Wisely, and slow; they stumble that run fast.

WILLIAM SHAKESPEARE (1564–1616)

Foul deeds will rise, though all the earth o'erwhelm them, to men's eyes.

WILLIAM SHAKESPEARE (1564–1616)

He that can have patience can have what he will.

BENJAMIN FRANKLIN (1706–1790)

Austere perseverance, harsh and continuous, may be employed by the least of us and rarely fails of its purpose, for its silent power grows irresistibly greater with time.

JOHANN WOLFGANG VON GOETHE (1749–1832)

You never know what is enough unless you know what is more than enough.

WILLIAM BLAKE (1757–1827)

We must dare, and dare again, and go on daring.

GEORGES JACQUES DANTON (1759–1794)

The best-laid schemes o' mice an' men gang aft a-gley.

ROBERT BURNS (1759–1796)

Circumstances—what are circumstances? I make circumstances.

NAPOLEON BONAPARTE (1769–1821)

Our grand business in life is not to see what lies dimly at a distance, but to do what lies clearly at hand.

THOMAS CARLYLE (1795–1881)

Every noble work is at first impossible.

THOMAS CARLYLE (1795–1881)

Be ashamed to die until you have won some victory for humanity.

HORACE MANN (1796–1859)

Nothing great was ever achieved without enthusiasm.

RALPH WALDO EMERSON (1803 1882)

Keep cool: it will all be over 100 years hence.

RALPH WALDO EMERSON (1803–1882)

Everything comes if a man will only wait.

BENJAMIN DISRAELI (1804–1881)

We are not creatures of circumstance; we are creators of circumstance.

BENJAMIN DISRAELI (1804–1881)

Every production of genius must be the production of enthusiasm.

BENJAMIN DISRAELI (1804–1881)

I am in earnest; I will not equivocate; I will not excuse; I will not retreat a single inch; and I will be heard.

WILLIAM LLOYD GARRISON (1805–1879)

Perseverance is a great element of success. If you only knock long enough and loud enough at the gate, you are sure to wake up somebody.

HENRY WADSWORTH LONGFELLOW (1807–1882)

The great thing in this world is not so much where we are, but in what direction we are moving.

OLIVER WENDELL HOLMES (1809–1894)

To strive, to seek, to find, and not to yield.

ALFRED LORD TENNYSON (1809–1892)

Always bear in mind that your own resolution to
success is more important than any other one thing.

ABRAHAM LINCOLN (1809–1865)

Would you have your songs endure? Build on the
human heart.

ROBERT BROWNING (1812–1889)

'Tis not what man does which exalts him, but what
man would do.

ROBERT BROWNING (1812–1889)

The greatest discovery of my generation is that a
human being can alter his life by altering his
attitudes of mind.

WILLIAM JAMES (1842–1910)

To improve the golden moment of opportunity, and
catch the good that is within our reach, is the great
art of life.

WILLIAM JAMES (1842–1910)

Men habitually use only a small part of the powers
which they possess and which they might use under
appropriate circumstances.

WILLIAM JAMES (1842–1910)

■

In any project the important factor is your belief.
Without belief there can be no successful outcome.

WILLIAM JAMES (1842–1910)

■

He who would be great anywhere must first be great
in his own Philadelphia.

RUSSELL H. CONWELL (1843–1925)

■

I prefer the folly of enthusiasm to the indifference of
wisdom.

ANATOLE FRANCE (1844–1924)

■

Whatever you attempt, go at it with spirit. Put some
in!

DAVID STARR JORDAN (1851–1931)

■

Be strong!
It matters not how deep entrenched the wrong

How hard the battle goes, the day how long
Faint not—fight on! Tomorrow comes the song.

MALTBIE D. BABCOCK (1858–1901)

Destiny is not a matter of chance; it is a matter of
choice. It is not a thing to be waited for; it is a thing
to be achieved.

WILLIAM JENNINGS BRYAN (1860–1925)

A man can succeed at almost anything for which he
has unlimited enthusiasm.

CHARLES M. SCHWAB (1862–1939)

The more things change, the more they remain the
same.

FRENCH PROVERB

The thing always happens that you really believe in;
and the belief in a thing makes it happen.

FRANK LLOYD WRIGHT (1869–1959)

Whatever you do, put romance and enthusiasm into
the life of our children.

MARGARET RAMSEY MACDONALD (1870–1911)

Never, never, never, never give up.

WINSTON CHURCHILL (1874–1965)

The real secret of success is enthusiasm. Yes, more than enthusiasm, I would say excitement. I like to see men get excited. When they get excited they make a success of their lives.

WALTER CHRYSLER (1875–1940)

God will help you if you try, and you can if you think you can.

ANNA DELANEY PEALE (1875–1939)

If a door slams shut it means that God is pointing to an open door further on down.

ANNA DELANEY PEALE (1875–1939)

Enthusiasm is a kind of faith that has been set afire.

GEORGE MATTHEW ADAMS (1878–1962)

The world is moving so fast these days that the man who says it can't be done is generally interrupted by someone doing it.

HARRY EMERSON FOSDICK (1878–1968)

One can never consent to creep when one feels an
impulse to soar.

HELEN KELLER (1880–1968)

My mother said to me, "If you become a soldier
you'll be a general; if you become a monk you'll end
up as the pope." Instead, I became a painter and
wound up as Picasso.

PABLO PICASSO (1881–1973)

Somebody said that it couldn't be done
But he with a chuckle replied
That "maybe it couldn't," but he would be one
Who wouldn't say so till he'd tried.

EDGAR A. GUEST (1881–1959)

To be happy, drop the words *if only* and substitute
instead the words *next time.*

SMILEY BLANTON, M.D. (1882–1966)

Once a decision was made I did not worry about it
afterward.

HARRY S TRUMAN (1884–1972)

The future belongs to those who believe in the
beauty of their dreams.

ELEANOR ROOSEVELT (1884–1962)

Take calculated risks. That is quite different from
being rash.

GEORGE S. PATTON (1885–1945)

Flaming enthusiasm, backed up by horse sense and
persistence, is the quality that most frequently
makes for success.

DALE CARNEGIE (1888–1955)

You can be an ordinary athlete by getting away with
less than your best. But if you want to be a great,
you have to give it all you've got—your everything.

DUKE P. KAHANAMOKU (1890–1968)

I rate enthusiasm even above professional skill.

SIR EDWARD APPLETON (1892–1965)

An enthusiast may bore others, but he has never a
dull moment himself.

JOHN KIERAN (1892–1981)

He was a *how* thinker, not an *if* thinker.

ANONYMOUS

Four steps to achievement: plan purposefully, prepare prayerfully, proceed positively, pursue persistently.

WILLIAM A. WARD (1893–1959)

Act as if it were impossible to fail.

DOROTHEA BRANDE (1893–1948)

Roy has a great asset—20 percent vision. He wears thick glasses with an extra strong lens. So he never sees an obstacle in his path and goes on to success.

JOHN TIGRETT ON PUBLISHER ROY THOMSON (1894–1976)

Hell is the place where one has ceased to hope.

A. J. CRONIN (1896–1981)

There ain't nothing from the outside can lick any of us.

MARGARET MITCHELL (1900–1949), IN *Gone with the Wind*

Man is not the sum of what he has but the totality
of what he does not yet have, of what he might have.

JEAN PAUL SARTRE (1905–1980)

We must dare to think unthinkable thoughts.

JAMES W. FULBRIGHT (1905–   )

Find a need and fill it.

RUTH STAFFORD PEALE (1906–   )

If we really want to live, we'd better start at once to
try.

W.H. AUDEN (1907–1973)

Victory is not won in miles but in inches. Win a
little now, hold your ground, and later win a little
more.

LOUIS L'AMOUR (1908–1988)

We always teach employees to have positive
attitudes toward people and to their work.

RONNIE MORRIS (1911–1989)

Every problem contains the seeds of its own solution.

STANLEY ARNOLD (1925–   )

■

Shoot for the moon. Even if you miss it you will land among the stars.

LES BROWN (1928–   )

■

I want this team to win. I'm obsessed with winning, with discipline, with achieving.

GEORGE STEINBRENNER (1930–   )

■

They never told me I couldn't.

TOM DEMPSEY (1947–   )

■

Don't wait for your ship to come; swim out to it.

ANONYMOUS

■

Be bold   and mighty forces will come to your aid

BASIL KING (1859–1928)

Every man is enthusiastic at times. One man has
enthusiasm for thirty minutes, another has it for
thirty days—but it is the man that has it for thirty
years who makes a success in life.

THE CATHOLIC LAYMAN

Every tomorrow has two handles. You can take hold
of the handle of anxiety or the handle of enthusiasm.
Upon your choice so will be the day.

ANONYMOUS

Three
God's Creation

One of the happiest men I ever knew was Bill Stidger, a professor, preacher, and writer. He always seemed to be bubbling over with joy and enthusiasm. I remember having some oyster stew with him in the South Station, Boston, and asking him why he was so full of happiness.

He told me that it was because he practiced the attitude of gratitude. "When I wake up in the morning," he said, "I thank the Lord for a sound night's sleep. I give thanks for my wife and children, for the work I have to do, for my friends and opportunities. I just run over the world in my mind, thanking him for the wonderful things in it."

I guarantee that no one can be dull or blasé with such an attitude. And what marvelous things there are for which to be grateful in God's great Creation! My wife, Ruth, and I like to travel. I experience a kind of rebirth every time I think about some of the fascinating places we have visited: Japan with its vibrant aliveness; the green island of Formosa lying in the azure sea; the Philippines and the golden sunlight there; the profound serenity of the great forests of Australia; the breathtaking grandeur of the Swiss mountains; the lovable charm of England; and the beautiful vastness of America, from New England to the Deep South, the Grand Canyon, Alaska, and the matchless Hawaiian Islands.

But above all I am thankful for people like you, the reader of this book, for you are a creation of God unequaled anywhere in the universe. God never made anyone else exactly like you, and he never will again. Thank him for yourself and then for all the rest of his glorious handiwork.

And God saw every thing that he had made, and, behold, it was very good.

GENESIS 1:31

The earth is the Lord's, and the fulness thereof.

PSALM 24:1

The earth is full of the goodness of the Lord.

PSALM 33:5

O Lord, how manifold are thy works! in wisdom hast
thou made them all.

PSALM 104:24

We are his workmanship.

EPHESIANS 2:10

Thou has created all things, and for thy pleasure they
are and were created.

REVELATION 4:11

April hath put a spirit of youth in every thing.

WILLIAM SHAKESPEARE (1564–1616)

Night's candles are burnt out, and jocund day
Stands tiptoe on the misty mountain tops.

WILLIAM SHAKESPEARE (1564–1616)

The sky is the daily bread of the eyes.

RALPH WALDO EMERSON (1803–1882)

The splendor falls on castle walls
And snowy summits old in story
The long light shakes across the lakes
And the wild cataract leaps in glory.

ALFRED LORD TENNYSON (1809–1892)

■

The gathering orange stain
Upon the edge of yonder western peak
Reflects the sunsets of a thousand years.

ANONYMOUS

■

I must go down to the seas again,
To the lonely sea and the sky,
And all I ask is a tall ship and a star
To steer her by.

JOHN MASEFIELD (1878–1967).

■

A sense of curiosity is nature's original school of
education.

SMILEY BLANTON, M.D. (1882–1966)

Poems are made by fools like me,
But only God can make a tree.

JOYCE KILMER (1886–1918)

It's a beautiful day for it.

DAILY COMMENT OF WILBUR CROSS (1862–1948)

Syracuse weather consists of eleven months of
winter and one month of poor sleighing.

SAYING IN SYRACUSE, NEW YORK (CA. 1920)

Spring is God's way of saying, "One more time!"

ROBERT ORBEN (1927–   )

Four
Faith

One of my favorite places is the little Swiss village of Burgenstock, near Lucerne. It is such a charming mixture of farms, cottages, shops, and hotels that it captures the essence of Swiss beauty and efficiency.

Burgenstock is pervaded by the spirit of a remarkable man named Friedrich Frey, who developed it. Born a peasant, Frey became an important figure in the Swiss power industry and then one of the greatest hotelkeepers in the world. His son Fritz once surprised me with the statement that his father's greatness arose out of a youthful sickness that required him to spend a year in the hospital. When I asked Fritz how that experience led to greatness, he said, "During that year my father read the Bible six times."

From that, Fritz said, his father developed such a faith that, if he were to walk a ridge with steep precipices on both sides, he would do it absolutely without fear: "He was never afraid of anything after the time he poured the Bible down inside himself."

For me, faith is another word for positive thinking. When real faith grips you, you develop a mind-set that looks for the best in everything, refuses to give up, finds a way around (or through) every obstacle, and presses on to victory. Such faith is the consequence of "pouring down inside yourself" the great truths of the Bible and thus being triumphant in human experience.

The quotations in this section, as you make them a vital part of your thoughts and actions, will help you to live positively and triumphantly.

God is our refuge and strength, a very present help in trouble.

PSALM 46:1

Be still, and know that I am God.

PSALM 46:10

Let us hear the conclusion of the whole matter: Fear God, and keep his commandments: for this is the whole duty of man.

ECCLESIASTES 12:13

Where your treasure is, there will your heart be also.

MATTHEW 6:21

If ye have faith as a grain of mustard seed . . .
nothing shall be impossible unto you.

MATTHEW 17:20

All things are possible to him that believeth.

MARK 9:23

The things which are impossible with men are
possible with God.

LUKE 18:27

I am come that they might have life, and that they
might have it more abundantly.

JOHN 10:10

If it were not so, I would have told you.

JOHN 14:2

If God be for us, who can be against us?

ROMANS 8:31

Eye hath not seen, nor ear heard, neither have
entered into the heart of man, the things which God
hath prepared for them that love him.

1 CORINTHIANS 2:9

Faith is the substance of things hoped for, the
evidence of things not seen.

HEBREWS 11:1

Men willingly believe what they wish.

JULIUS CAESAR (102–44 B.C.)

The one thing worth living for is to keep one's soul
pure.

MARCUS AURELIUS (121–180)

For the multitude of worldly friends profiteth not,
nor may strong helpers anything avail, nor wise
counselors give profitable counsel, nor the cunning of
doctors give consolation, nor riches deliver in time of
need, nor a secret place defend, if Thou, Lord, do not
assist, help, comfort, counsel, inform, and defend.

THOMAS À KEMPIS (1380–1471)

Great and wonderful are thy works, Almighty God.

MOUNTAINTOP PLAQUE, SWITZERLAND

A mighty fortress is our God,
A bulwark never failing;
Our helper he amid the flood
Of mortal ills prevailing.

MARTIN LUTHER (1483–1546)

Let nothing disturb you, let nothing frighten you:
everything passes away except God; God alone is
sufficient.

ST. THERESA (1515–1582)

Two things fill the mind with ever increasing
wonder and awe . . . the starry heavens above me and
the moral law within me.

IMMANUEL KANT (1724–1804)

The writers against religion, whilst they oppose
every system, are wisely careful never to set up any
of their own.

EDMUND BURKE (1729–1797)

God moves in a mysterious way
His wonders to perform;
He plants his footsteps in the sea
And rides upon the storm.

WILLIAM COWPER (1731–1800)

■

What the inner voice says will not disappoint the
hoping soul.

JOHANN CHRISTOPH FRIEDRICH VON SCHILLER (1759–1805)

■

In God we trust.

MOTTO ON U.S. CURRENCY

■

Truth, crushed to earth, shall rise again;
The eternal years of God are hers;
But Error, wounded, writhes in pain,
And dies among his worshipers.

WILLIAM CULLEN BRYANT (1794–1878)

■

Before me, even as behind,
God is, and all is well.

JOHN GREENLEAF WHITTIER (1807–1892)

God asks no man whether he will accept life. This is not the choice. You must take it. The only question is how.

HENRY WARD BEECHER (1813–1887)

God gives us always strength enough, and sense enough, for every thing he wants us to do.

JOHN RUSKIN (1819–1900)

Fear knocked at the door.
Faith answered.
No one was there.

OLD SAYING

The light of God surrounds me,
The love of God enfolds me,
The power of God protects me,
The Presence of God watches over me,
Wherever I am, God is.

PRAYER CARD

Ten minutes spent in Christ's society every day, aye two minutes, will make the whole day different.

HENRY DRUMMOND (1851–1897)

41

Every day affirm: I am never alone. I can do my job well. With God's help I can succeed. I am a positive thinker and believer.

JOHN GLOSSINGER (1868–?)

Always remember and never forget it: Jesus Christ can make men and women what they can be.

CHARLES CLIFFORD PEALE (1870–1955)

Every morning I spend fifteen minutes filling my mind full of God; and so there's no room left for worry thoughts.

HOWARD CHANDLER CHRISTY (1873–1952)

It may be that each individual consciousness is a brain cell in a universal mind.

SIR JAMES JEANS (1877–1946)

I am full-fed and yet I hunger. What means this deeper hunger in my heart?

ALFRED NOYES (1880–1958)

We have only to believe, then little by little we shall see the universal horror unbend and then smile upon us.

PIERRE TEILHARD DE CHARDIN (1881–1955)

The first and finest lesson that parents can teach their children is faith and courage.

SMILEY BLANTON, M.D. (1882–1966)

A power greater than any human being helped make this decision.

HERBERT J. STIEFEL (1917–   )

Boys, this is only a game. But it's like life in that you will be dealt some bad hands. Take each hand, good or bad, and don't whine and complain but play it out. If you're men enough to do that, God will help and you will come out well.

DWIGHT D. EISENHOWER (1890–1969), QUOTING HIS MOTHER

The soul can split the sky in two, and let the face of God shine through.

EDNA ST. VINCENT MILLAY (1892–1950)

We have grasped the mystery of the atom and
rejected the Sermon on the Mount.

OMAR N. BRADLEY (1893–1986)

I learned really to practice mustard seed faith, and
positive thinking, and remarkable things happened.

SIR JOHN WALTON (1904–   )

Think of only three things—your God, your family,
and the Green Bay Packers—in that order.

VINCE LOMBARDI (1913–1970), TO HIS TEAM

Now you just believe. That is all you have to do; just
believe.

ADVICE FROM AN OLD OHIO FARMER

The Bible tells us that a sparrow does not fall
without God's notice. I know he will help us meet
our responsibilities through his guidance.

MICHAEL CARDONE, SR. (1917–   )

Given willpower enough and brains enough and faith
enough, almost anything can be done.

ANONYMOUS ENGINEER

Five
Prayer

There are three principal ways to get what we need: by work, by thought, and by prayer. Most people work hard, and some utilize the power of thought. But prayer is greatly neglected. And this is unfortunate, for the most powerful energy one can generate is prayer energy.

How does a person acquire this energy? The first step is simply to pray. As a young man, I was interested in public speaking and listened to some of the greatest orators of my time. Once, after a particularly rousing masterpiece of clocution, I asked the speaker how one could become proficient in that art. His answer was, "By speaking." He explained: "Learn by doing. Speak every time you get a chance. Keep doing it. Practice constantly, seeking to improve your ability."

The best way to learn anything is by doing.

If you want to utilize the matchless power of prayer, begin praying immediately and continue at every opportunity. I have observed from a number of inquiries that the average person probably spends about five minutes a day in prayer. That is one half of 1 percent of one's waking hours. Back in the days of Prohibition in the United States, half of 1 percent of alcohol was declared by act of Congress to be nonintoxicating. That percentage is also nonintoxicating in religion! If you want to experience the heady energy of prayer, practice it more often.

The physician Alexis Carrel, a spiritual pioneer, advised praying everywhere: in the street, the office, the shop, the school. You can transform spare moments by praying for your needs, for those around you, for your friends and loved ones, for everyone and everything you can think of. Then believe that your prayers will be answered. They will be. And prayer is always answered in one of three ways: no, yes, or wait awhile.

What things soever ye desire, when ye pray, believe that ye receive them, and ye shall have them.

MARK 11:24

■

Ye have not, because ye ask not.

JAMES 4:2

Lord, I shall be very busy this day. I may forget thee, but do not thou forget me.

SIR JACOB ASTLEY (ELEVENTH CENTURY)

My words fly up, my thoughts stay below;
Words without thoughts never to heaven go.

WILLIAM SHAKESPEARE (1564–1616)

Work as if you were to live 100 years; pray as if you were to die tomorrow.

BENJAMIN FRANKLIN (1706–1790)

I who still pray at morning and at eve
Thrice in my life perhaps have truly prayed,
Thrice stirred below conscious self
Have felt that perfect disenthrallment which is God.

JAMES RUSSELL LOWELL (1819–1891)

Prayer is a cry of distress, a demand for help, a hymn of love.

ALEXIS CARREL (1873–1944)

Prayer, like radium, is a luminous and self-generating form of energy.

ALEXIS CARREL (1873–1944)

When we pray we link ourselves with an inexhaustible motive power.

ALEXIS CARREL (1873–1944)

When I have a problem I pray about it, and what comes to mind and stays there I assume to be my answer. And this has been right so often that I know it is God's answer.

J. L. KRAFT (1874–1953)

God listens to our weeping when the occasion itself is beyond our knowledge but still within his love and power.

DANIEL A. POLING (1884–1968)

Prayer may not change things for you, but it for sure changes you for things.

SAMUEL M. SHOEMAKER (1893–1963)

Prayer begins where human capacity ends.

MARIAN ANDERSON (1902–   )

■

There are three answers to prayer: yes, no, and wait awhile. It must be recognized that no is an answer.

RUTH STAFFORD PEALE (1906–   )

■

Visualize, "prayerize," "actionize," and your wishes will come true.

CHARLES L. ALLEN (1913–   )

Six
Relationships

———■———

Wₑ hear so much about relationships today that one might get the idea that this is a twentieth-century concept. Actually, the importance of good relationships has been known throughout history.

The great Rabbi Hillel (30 B.C.–A.D. 10) was once asked if he could sum up the Jewish law while standing on one foot. He answered: "Do not unto others that which you would not have them do unto you. That is the entire Torah; the rest is commentary." And the ancient law codes of Babylon and China revolve primarily around just and fair relationships.

But our relationships with other people remain today one of our greatest problems. The president of a large company once told me that the most important thing in his business was the relationships among the employees.

During one of Billy Graham's evangelistic crusades in London, the British newspapers quoted some cutting remarks about him by a well-known clergyman of that country. It was reported that when someone began telling Billy about this, he said: "God bless that man. If I were in his place, I'd probably feel the same way about me." Such an attitude ensures personal peace of mind as well as the love and respect of other people.

Mahatma Gandhi spent his whole life helping his fellow citizens achieve their independence. What it took George Washington seven years of bloody war to accomplish, Gandhi did over more than thirty years by the power of quiet, loving nonresistance.

Jesus made it clear that the most important thing in the world is our relationship to God and to others. When we achieve that, everything good will follow.

Hatred stirreth up strifes: but love covereth all sins.

PROVERBS 10:12

A bad neighbor is a misfortune, as much as a good one is a great blessing.

HESIOD (EIGHTH CENTURY B.C.)

Once harm has been done, even a fool understands it.

HOMER (1200–850 B.C.)

What you do not want done to yourself, do not do to
others.

CONFUCIUS (551–479 B.C.)

It is in the character of very few men to honor
without envy a friend who has prospered.

AESCHYLUS (525–456 B.C.)

A lie never lives to be old.

SOCRATES (469–399 B.C.)

We secure our friends not by accepting favors but by
doing them.

THUCYDIDES (460–400 B.C.)

We should behave to our friends as we would wish
our friends to behave to us.

ARISTOTLE (384–322 B.C.)

The shifts of fortune test the reliability of friends.

MARCUS TULLIUS CICERO (106–43 B.C.)

53

Once a word has been allowed to escape, it cannot be
recalled.

HORACE (QUINTUS HORATIUS FLACCUS, 65–8 B.C.)

Grant that we may not so much seek to be
understood as to understand.

ST. FRANCIS OF ASSISI (1182–1266)

This above all: to thine own self be true;
And it must follow, as the night the day,
Thou canst not then be false to any man.

WILLIAM SHAKESPEARE (1564–1616)

Teach me, my God and King, in all things thee to
see, and what I do in any thing, to do it as for thee.

GEORGE HERBERT (1593–1633)

Do all the good you can,
By all the means you can,
In all the ways you can,
In all the places you can,
At all the times you can,

To all the people you can,
As long as ever you can.

JOHN WESLEY (1703–1791)

Trust not him with your secrets, who left alone in
your room, turns over your papers.

JOHANN KASPAR LAVATER (1741–1801)

Common-looking people are the best in the world:
that is the reason the Lord makes so many of them.

ABRAHAM LINCOLN (1809–1865)

To look up and not down,
To look forward and not back,
To look out and not in, and
To lend a hand.

EDWARD EVERETT HALE (1822–1909)

Nothing is ever lost by courtesy. It is the cheapest of
pleasures, costs nothing, and conveys much. It
pleases him who gives and receives and thus, like
mercy, is twice blessed.

ERASTUS WIMAN (1834–1904)

There is no happiness in having or in getting, but
only in giving.

HENRY DRUMMOND (1851–1897)

Too many people do not care what happens as long
as it does not happen to them.

WILLIAM HOWARD TAFT (1857–1930)

Example is not the main thing in influencing others.
It is the only thing.

ALBERT SCHWEITZER (1875–1965)

You give but little when you give of your
possessions. It is when you give of yourself that you
truly give.

KAHLIL GIBRAN (1883–1931)

Conscience is the perfect interpreter of life.

KARL BARTH (1886–1968)

Do things for others and you'll find your
self-consciousness evaporating like morning dew on a
Missouri cornfield in July.

DALE CARNEGIE (1888–1955)

You can make more friends in two months by
becoming more interested in other people than you
can in two years by trying to get people interested in
you.

DALE CARNEGIE (1888–1955)

There can be no daily democracy without daily
citizenship.

RALPH NADER (1934–   )

Seven
Self

Although most of us probably attribute our problems to other people or to bad luck or to the circumstances around us, the truth is that we create our own success or failure. The road to successful, positive living begins with an analysis of ourselves and depends ultimately on how we think of ourselves.

Years ago I wrote: "Without a humble but reasonable confidence in your own powers you cannot succeed. But with sound self-confidence you can succeed. A sense of inferiority and inadequacy interferes with the attainment of your hopes, but self-confidence leads to self-realization and successful achievement" (*The Power of Positive Thinking*). Now, more than ever, I am convinced that this is true.

How do you build confidence in yourself? Take your mind off the things that seem to be against you. Thinking about negative factors simply builds them up into a power they need not have. Instead, mentally affirm and reaffirm and visualize your assets—the love of God your Father, the ability of your mind and talents, the goodwill of your friends and family, your physical health, your strengths, your future, your possibilities. Stamp indelibly on your mind a picture of yourself succeeding. Make an accurate estimate of your ability, then raise it 10 percent. Affirm that God is with you. Put yourself in his hands and believe that you are now receiving power from him for all your needs.

Read the statements that follow and make them part of yourself. You will learn how to better control your thought processes and, ultimately, your destiny.

Thou shalt love thy neighbor as thyself.

LEVITICUS 19:18

There is a spirit in man: and the inspiration of the Almighty giveth them understanding.

JOB 32:8

He restoreth my soul.

PSALM 23:3

Bless the Lord, O my soul: and all that is within me,
bless his holy name.

PSALM 103:1

I am fearfully and wonderfully made.

PSALM 139:14

Say to them that are of a fearful heart, Be strong, fear
not.

ISAIAH 35:4

We would often be sorry if our wishes were gratified.

AESOP (620–560 B.C.)

The destiny of man is in his own soul.

HERODOTUS (FIFTH CENTURY B.C.)

Life is to be in relations.

LAO-TZU (FIFTH CENTURY B.C.)

Numberless are the world's wonders but none more
wonderful than man.

SOPHOCLES (496–406 B.C.)

Often when looking at a mass of things for sale, he would say to himself, "How many things I have no need of."

SOCRATES (469–399 B.C.)

The life which is unexamined is not worth living.

PLATO (427–347 B.C.)

Nothing is easier than self-deceit.

DEMOSTHENES (384–322 B. C.)

Sincerity is the way to heaven.

MENCIUS (371–288 B.C.)

Yield not to evil, but attack all the more boldly.

VIRGIL (PUBLIUS VERGILIUS MARO, 70–19 B.C.)

A good reputation is more valuable than money.

PUBLILIUS SYRUS (CA. 42 B.C.)

You can tell the character of every man when you see how he receives praise.

LUCIUS ANNAEUS SENECA (4 B.C.–A.D. 65)

By their fruits ye shall know them.

MATTHEW 7:20

What shall it profit a man, if he shall gain the whole
world, and lose his own soul?

MARK 8:36

If ye know these things, happy are ye if ye do them.

JOHN 13:17

Put on the new man, which after God is created in
righteousness and true holiness.

EPHESIANS 4:24

I can do all things through Christ which
strengtheneth me.

PHILIPPIANS 4:13

With man most of his misfortunes are occasioned by
man.

PLINY THE ELDER (23–79)

The first rule is to keep an untroubled spirit. The second is to look things in the face and know them for what they are.

MARCUS AURELIUS (121–180)

Man must be arched and buttressed from within, else the temple wavers to the dust.

MARCUS AURELIUS (121–180)

Our life is what our thoughts make of it.

MARCUS AURELIUS (121–180)

To live each day as though one's last, never flustered, never apathetic, never attitudinizing—here is the perfection of character.

MARCUS AURELIUS (121–180)

A cheerful look makes a dish a feast.

AURELIUS CLEMENS PRUDENTIUS (346–410)

To go against one's conscience is neither safe nor right. Here I stand. I cannot do otherwise.

MARTIN LUTHER (1483–1546)

He got the better of himself, and that's the best kind
of victory one can wish for.

MIGUEL DE CERVANTES (1546–1611)

A man of words and not of deeds is like a garden full
of weeds.

ANONYMOUS

The fault, dear Brutus, is not in our stars
But in ourselves that we are underlings.

WILLIAM SHAKESPEARE (1564–1616)

Assume a virtue, if you have it not.

WILLIAM SHAKESPEARE (1564–1616)

His life was gentle, and the elements
So mixed in him that might stand up and say
To all the world, "This was a man!"

WILLIAM SHAKESPEARE (1564–1616)

Every man's work, whether it be literature, or music, or pictures, or architecture, or anything else, is always a portrait of himself.

SAMUEL BUTLER (1612–1680)

I do all my actions in the sight of God, who must judge of them, and to whom I have consecrated them all.

BLAISE PASCAL (1623–1662)

Do not weep; do not wax indignant. Understand.

BARUCH SPINOZA (1632–1677)

Cheerfulness keeps up a kind of daylight in the mind, and fills it with a steady and perpetual serenity.

JOSEPH ADDISON (1672–1719)

Genius is nothing but a greater aptitude for patience.

BENJAMIN FRANKLIN (1706–1790)

Dost thou love life? Then do not squander time, for that's the stuff life is made of.

BENJAMIN FRANKLIN (1706–1790)

I agree that there is a natural aristocracy among men.
The grounds of this are virtue and talents.

THOMAS JEFFERSON (1743–1826)

As soon as you trust yourself, you will know how to
live.

JOHANN WOLFGANG VON GOETHE (1749–1832)

He who has a firm will molds the world to himself.

JOHANN WOLFGANG VON GOETHE (1749–1832)

Let us not forget that a man can never get away from
himself.

JOHANN WOLFGANG VON GOETHE (1749–1832)

Talent develops itself in solitude; character in the
stream of life.

JOHANN WOLFGANG VON GOETHE (1749–1832)

One ought every day at least to hear a little song,
read a good poem, see a fine picture, and, if it were
possible, to speak a few reasonable words.

JOHANN WOLFGANG VON GOETHE (1749–1832)

67

The good things of life are not to be had singly but come to us with a mixture.

CHARLES LAMB (1775–1834)

To live content with small means; to seek elegance rather than luxury, and refinement rather than fashion; to be worthy, not respectable, and wealthy, not rich; to study hard, think quietly, talk gently, act frankly; to listen to the stars and birds, to babes and sages, with open heart; to bear on cheerfully, do all bravely, awaiting occasions, worry never; in a word to, like the spiritual, unbidden and unconscious, grow up through the common.

WILLIAM ELLERY CHANNING (1780–1842)

Give me a man who sings at his work.

THOMAS CARLYLE (1795–1881)

Alas! the fearful unbelief is unbelief in yourself.

THOMAS CARLYLE (1795–1881)

Silence is the element in which great things fashion themselves together.

THOMAS CARLYLE (1795–1881)

Nothing can bring you peace but yourself.

RALPH WALDO EMERSON (1803 – 1882)

■

A man is a method, a progressive arrangement; a selecting principle, gathering his like unto him wherever he goes. What you are comes to you.

RALPH WALDO EMERSON (1803 – 1882)

■

Nature arms each man with some faculty which enables him to do easily some feat impossible to any other.

RALPH WALDO EMERSON (1803 – 1882)

■

Self-trust is the first secret of success.

RALPH WALDO EMERSON (1803 – 1882)

■

A man is what he thinks about all day long.

RALPH WALDO EMERSON (1803 – 1882)

■

The world belongs to the energetic.

RALPH WALDO EMERSON (1803 – 1882)

Make the most of yourself for that is all there is to you.

RALPH WALDO EMERSON (1803–1882)

The secret to success in life is for a man to be ready for his opportunity when it comes.

BENJAMIN DISRAELI (1804–1881)

In character, in manner, in style, in all things, the supreme excellence is simplicity.

HENRY WADSWORTH LONGFELLOW (1807–1882)

Self-reverence, self-knowledge, self-control. These three alone lead life to sovereign power.

ALFRED LORD TENNYSON (1809–1892)

Grateful for the blessing lent of simple tastes and mind content!

OLIVER WENDELL HOLMES (1809–1894)

What a man thinks of himself, that it is which determines or rather indicates his fate.

HENRY DAVID THOREAU (1817–1862)

Blessed is the man who, having nothing to say,
abstains from giving in words evidence of the fact.

GEORGE ELIOT (MARY ANN EVANS, 1819–1880)

Mishaps are like knives, that either serve us or cut
us, as we grasp them by the blade or the handle.

JAMES RUSSELL LOWELL (1819–1891)

Tell yourself in your secret reveries, I was made to
handle affairs.

ANDREW CARNEGIE (1835–1919)

Men habitually use only a small part of the power
they possess and which they might use under
appropriate circumstances.

WILLIAM JAMES (1842–1910)

If you want a quality, act as if you already had it. Try
the "as if" technique.

WILLIAM JAMES (1842–1910)

I am the master of my fate; I am the captain of my
soul.

WILLIAM ERNEST HENLEY (1849–1903)

A man is literally what he thinks.

JAMES ALLEN (1849–1925)

■

Sit loosely in the saddle of life.

ROBERT LOUIS STEVENSON (1850–1894)

■

A man can stand a lot as long as he can stand himself.

AXEL MUNTHE (1857–1949)

■

All the resources we need are in the mind.

THEODORE ROOSEVELT, JR. (1858–1919)

■

The bigger they come, the harder they fall.

BOB FITZSIMMONS (1862–1917)

■

We have forty million reasons for failure but not a single excuse.

RUDYARD KIPLING (1865–1936)

■

You are beaten to earth? Well, well, what's that?
Come up with a smiling face,

It's nothing against you to fall down flat
But to lie there — that's disgrace.

EDMUND VANCE COOKE (1866–1932)

I dare you to be the strongest boy in this class.

WILLIAM H. DANFORTH (1870–1955), QUOTING A TEACHER

We are what we believe we are.

BENJAMIN N. CARDOZO (1870–1938)

When I decided to go into politics I weighed the cost:
I would get criticism. But I went ahead. So when the
virulent criticism came I wasn't surprised. I was
better able to handle it.

HERBERT HOOVER (1874–1964)

Speech is silver; silence is golden.

SWISS PROVERB

Knock the *t* off the *can't*.

GEORGE REEVES (1876–1925)

We're all born under the same sky, but we don't all
have the same horizon.

KONRAD ADENAUER (1876–1967)

Don't ever say, "I can't." All you need is God and
gumption. You can if you think 'tis you.

A. HARRY MOORE (1879–1952), QUOTING HIS MOTHER

Three outstanding qualities make for success:
judgment, industry, health. And the greatest of these
is judgment.

WILLIAM MAXWELL AITKEN, LORD BEAVERBROOK (1879–1964)

Our life is at all times and before all else the
consciousness of what we can do.

JOSÉ ORTEGA Y GASSET (1883–1955)

Rancor is an outpouring of a feeling of inferiority.

JOSÉ ORTEGA Y GASSET (1883–1955)

It isn't life that matters; it's the courage you bring to
it.

HUGH WALPOLE (1884–1941)

Never build a case against yourself.

ROBERT ROWBOTTOM (1887–1973)

If you have to keep reminding yourself of a thing,
perhaps it isn't so.

CHRISTOPHER MORLEY (1890–1957)

Adversity causes some men to break; others to break
records.

WILLIAM A. WARD (1921–   )

Keep strong if possible; in any case keep cool.

SIR BASIL LIDDELL HART (1895–1970)

Our self-image strongly held essentially determines
what we become.

MAXWELL MALTZ (1899–1975)

When people are bored it is primarily with their own
selves that they are bored.

ERIC HOFFER (1902–1983)

To every disadvantage there is a corresponding
advantage.

W. CLEMENT STONE (1902–   )

The longest journey is the journey inward.

DAG HAMMARSKJÖLD (1905–1961)

I am somebody. I am me. I like being me. And I need
nobody to make me somebody.

LOUIS L'AMOUR (1908–1988)

A man can lose sight of everything else when he's
bent on revenge, and it ain't worth it.

LOUIS L'AMOUR (1908–1988)

Nothing in life is more exciting and rewarding than
the sudden flash of insight that leaves you a changed
person—not only changed, but for the better.

ARTHUR GORDON (1912–   )

Most people don't plan to fail; they fail to plan.

JOHN L. BECKLEY (1925–   )

We have left undone those things which we ought to
have done; and we have done those things which we
ought not to have done.

THE BOOK OF COMMON PRAYER

Eight
Physical Health

A few years ago, I clipped out a newspaper story about James A. Hard, who lived to the age of one hundred and eleven. One way this man cooperated with the forces of health and longevity, according to the paper, was by taking everything in stride. His friends said he was always happy. He never let himself get overly excited or upset, and he kept control of his life.

At the age of ninety, Mr. Hard had a cataract on one eye. His granddaughter said, "We were going to arrange to have an operation, but Grandpa beat us to it. All by himself, he went to a physician's office where he made the doctor perform the operation. Right after, he came home by himself in a cab. That was nothing but grit and courage."

Emotional tranquility, refusal to worry, the attitude of happiness, zest for life, keeping control, having grit and courage—these are important factors in physical health and long life.

Dr. Bernie S. Siegel of New Haven, Connecticut, believes, as many other physicians do today, that there is a close connection between health and mental attitudes. He sometimes asks his patients, "Why do you need this disease?" When they change their outlook, he reports, their health problems often end.

To practice the basic principles of good health, visualize yourself as sound, healthy and filled with the vitality and boundless life of your Creator. Look upon yourself as the unique individual that you are. Get in harmony with the creative, life-giving, health-maintaining forces of the universe. Affirm peace, wholeness, and good health—and they will be yours.

I am the Lord that healeth thee.

EXODUS 15:26

The Lord will take away from thee all sickness.

DEUTERONOMY 7:15

The Lord is the strength of my life.

PSALM 27:1

The tongue of the wise is health.

PROVERBS 12:18

A merry heart doeth good like a medicine.

PROVERBS 17:22

If a man insisted always on being serious, and never allowed himself a bit of fun and relaxation, he would go mad or become unstable without knowing it.

HERODOTUS (FIFTH CENTURY B.C.)

Those whom God wishes to destroy he first makes mad.

EURIPIDES (485–406 B.C.)

Beloved, I wish above all things that thou mayest prosper and be in health, even as thy soul prospereth.

3 JOHN 2

I am searching for that which every man seeks— peace and rest.

DANTE ALIGHIERI (1265–1321)

A well-spent day brings happy sleep.

LEONARDO DA VINCI (1452–1519)

Most of man's trouble comes from his inability to be
still.

BLAISE PASCAL (1623–1662)

Strange how a good dinner reconciles everybody.

SAMUEL PEPYS (1633–1703)

The best doctors in the world are Doctor Diet,
Doctor Quiet, and Dr. Merryman.

JONATHAN SWIFT (1667–1745)

Early to bed and early to rise,
Makes a man healthy, wealthy, and wise.

BENJAMIN FRANKLIN (1706–1790)

Do not worry, eat three square meals a day, say your
prayers, be courteous to your creditors, keep your
digestion good, exercise, go slow and easy.

ABRAHAM LINCOLN (1809–1865)

At the heart of a cyclone tearing the sky is a place of central calm.

EDWIN MARKHAM (1852–1940)

If you have arthritis, calmly say, "Okay, I have arthritis and this is the way arthritis is." Take pain, like people, as it comes and you can better master it.

CHARLES CLIFFORD PEALE (1870–1955)

The reason worry kills more people than work is that more people worry than work.

ROBERT FROST (1874–1963)

Practice easing your way along. Don't get het up or in a dither. Do your best; take it as it comes. You can handle anything if you think you can. Just keep your cool and your sense of humor.

SMILEY BLANTON, M.D. (1882–1966)

Faith is necessary for physical as well as spiritual well-being.

SMILEY BLANTON, M.D. (1882–1966)

I don't know why we are in such a hurry to get up when we fall down. You might think we would lie there and rest awhile.

MAX EASTMAN (1883–1969)

Hate and fear can poison the body as surely as any toxic chemicals.

JOSEPH KRIMSKY, M.D. (1883–?)

I come to the office each morning and stay for long hours doing what has to be done to the best of my ability. And when you've done the best you can, you can't do any better. So when I go to sleep I turn everything over to the Lord and forget it.

HARRY S TRUMAN (1884–1972)

We little realize the number of human diseases that are begun or affected by worry.

WALTER CLEMENT ALVAREZ, M.D. (1884–1978)

I have found that if you love life, life will love you back.

ARTHUR RUBINSTEIN (1887–1982)

Internal balance is health and internal unbalance is sickness.

CLARENCE COOK LITTLE, M.D. (1888–1971)

◾

To get the body in tone, get the mind in tune.

ZACHARY T. BERCOVITZ, M.D. (1895–1984)

◾

Some patients I see are actually draining into their bodies the diseased thoughts of their minds.

ZACHARY T. BERCOVITZ, M.D. (1895–1984)

◾

Worry affects the circulation, the heart, the glands, the whole nervous system, and profoundly affects heart action.

CHARLES W. MAYO, M.D. (1898–1968)

◾

Most of the time we think we're sick it's all in the mind.

THOMAS WOLFE (1900–1938)

◾

The best and most efficient pharmacy is within your own system.

ROBERT C. PEALE, M.D. (1900–1970)

I have become convinced that there is a definite
relationship between medical science and religious
faith and that God has given us both as weapons
against disease.

ROBERT C. PEALE, M.D. (1900–1970)

If you go long enough without a bath even the fleas
will let you alone.

ERNIE PYLE (1900–1945)

Many of my patients could have healthy hearts by
just practicing the therapy of their religion.

LOUIS F. BISHOP, M.D. (1901–1986)

I said to that high-strung patient, "Practice the peace
of God which passes all understanding and you will
be well."

LOUIS F. BISHOP, M.D. (1901–1986)

This is the age
Of the half-read page
And the quick hash
And the mad dash
The bright night

With the nerves tight
The plane hop
With the brief stop
The lamp tan
In a short span
The Big Shot
In a good spot
And the brain strain
And the heart pain
And the catnaps
Till the spring snaps
And the fun's done.

VIRGINIA BRASIER (1910–   )

Bacteria and other microorganisms find it easier to
infect people who worry and fret.

LEO RANGELL (1913–   )

Have you that gray sickness – half awake, half
asleep – half alive, half dead?

ADVERTISEMENT CAPTION

I told the doctors that God was my partner and I
believed he would help me walk again.

JANE WITHERS (1927–   ), WHEN PARALYZED

You can become strongest in your weakest place.

ANONYMOUS CONTEMPORARY

A clean engine always delivers power.

GAS STATION SIGN

Nine
Mental Health

At the bottom of the Great Depression of the 1930s I did a lot of counseling, trying to help many troubled people. As I attempted to meet the flood of need, I became aware of the role of unhealthy thought patterns in so many human problems. But I also realized my limitations in psychiatric knowledge, and I began searching for assistance in this important area.

In 1935, I met Dr. Smiley Blanton, one of the finest people I have ever known, skilled in spiritual as well as psychiatric wisdom and sensitivity. After I had told him of my search, Dr. Blanton surprised me by asking, "Do you believe in prayer?" When I assured him that I did, he said, "So do I," explaining that he had been praying for years that he would meet a pastor with whom he could work as a partner, uniting pastoral care with psychological science.

We formed such a team. At first, he counseled me about my problem cases. But he himself became increasingly involved, eventually bringing in young student psychiatrists to work with him. This work finally grew into the Institutes of Religion and Health, which now provide superior accredited training in pastoral counseling. Out of the institutes have developed more than a hundred pastoral counseling centers across the United States.

There is no doubt in my mind that mental and spiritual health are the foundation of physical health, harmonious relationships, and a happy and successful life. The quotations in this book may be thought of as prescriptions. Take one or more a day for increased courage and self-confidence.

The thing which I greatly feared is come upon me.

JOB 3:25

He healeth the broken in heart, and bindeth up their wounds.

PSALM 147:3

Thou wilt keep him in perfect peace, whose mind is
stayed on thee.

ISAIAH 26:3

Speech is like the cloth of Arras opened and spread
abroad, whereas in thought it lies in packs.

THEMISTOCLES (527–460 B.C.)

The greatest griefs are those we cause ourselves.

SOPHOCLES (496–406 B.C.)

There are two sides to every question.

PROTAGORAS (485–410 B.C.)

The mind is never right but when it is at peace
within itself.

LUCIUS ANNAEUS SENECA (4 B.C.–A.D. 65)

And be not conformed to this world: but be ye
transformed by the renewing of your mind.

ROMANS 12:2

Now the God of hope fill you with all joy and peace
in believing, that ye may abound in hope.

ROMANS 15:13

The peace of God, which passeth all understanding,
shall keep your hearts and minds through Christ
Jesus.

PHILIPPIANS 4:7

For God hath not given us the spirit of fear; but of
power, and of love, and of a sound mind.

2 TIMOTHY 1:7

Intellectual passion drives out sensuality.

LEONARDO DA VINCI (1452–1519)

Canst thou not minister to a mind diseased . . .
Raze out the written troubles of the brain? . . .
Therein the patient
Must minister to himself.

WILLIAM SHAKESPEARE (1564–1616)

The mind is its own place, and in itself can make a
heaven of hell, a hell of heaven.

JOHN MILTON (1608–1674)

Great men are they who see that the spiritual is
stronger than any material force; that thoughts rule
the world.

RALPH WALDO EMERSON (1803–1882)

Do the thing you fear and the death of fear is certain.

RALPH WALDO EMERSON (1803–1882)

Nothing is so much to be feared as fear.

HENRY DAVID THOREAU (1817–1862)

Let us be of good cheer, however, remembering that
the misfortunes hardest to bear are those which
never come.

JAMES RUSSELL LOWELL (1819–1891)

There is no more miserable human being than one in
whom nothing is habitual but indecision.

WILLIAM JAMES (1842–1910)

A great many people think they are thinking when
they are merely rearranging their prejudices.

WILLIAM JAMES (1842–1910)

Quiet minds cannot be perplexed or frightened but go
on in fortune or misfortune at their own private pace
like the ticking of a clock during a thunderstorm.

ROBERT LOUIS STEVENSON (1850–1894)

Laugh, and the world laughs with you; weep, and
you weep alone.

ELLA WHEELER WILCOX (1850–1919)

Some other faculty than the intellect is necessary for
the apprehension of reality.

HENRI BERGSON (1859–1941)

The only thing we have to fear is fear itself.

FRANKLIN DELANO ROOSEVELT (1882–1945)

Anxiety is the great modern plague. But faith can
cure it.

SMILEY BLANTON, M.D. (1882–1966)

Every day give yourself a good mental shampoo.

SARA JORDAN, M.D. (1884–1959)

If you want to conquer fear, don't sit at home and think about it. Go out and get busy.

DALE CARNEGIE (1888–1955)

I know only that what is moral is what you feel good after and what is immoral is what you feel bad after.

ERNEST HEMINGWAY (1899–1961)

Positive thinking is the key to success in business, education, pro football, anything that you can mention. I go out there thinking that I am going to complete every pass.

RON JAWORSKI (1951–   )

Ten
Pain and Suffering

P ain and suffering have wracked humanity throughout history. Evidence of arthritis has been discovered in the earliest skeletons of the past.

My friend Lloyd Ogilvie, distinguished pastor of the First Presbyterian Church of Hollywood, California, once said that he had learned several important lessons from personally experiencing pain and suffering. He found he grew the most spiritually during those ordeals. Another lesson was that, on looking back on such an experience afterward, he discovered it had deepened his trust in God. As a result, says Dr. Ogilvie, he is now able to thank God in advance for the prospect of such trials, praying, in effect, "Lord, thank you for the good that is going to happen in and through me as a result of what I am about to experience."

No one welcomes pain. But, rightly faced, it can bring about great good. And we can triumph over it. The day before the January 1988 Superbowl football game, Doug Williams, quarterback for the Washington Redskins, had to endure hours of dental surgery. During the game, his knee was injured. But he led the Redskins to victory in spite of his problems, breaking one record after another. No wonder he was named most valuable player that year!

When pain strikes, we often ask the wrong questions, such as, Why me? The right questions are, What can I learn from this? What can I do about it? What can I accomplish in spite of it?

Bring pain or suffering to the One who suffered for us on a cross and you will find "what a friend we have in Jesus."

Weeping may endure for a night, but joy cometh in the morning.

PSALM 30:5

∎

The pain of the mind is worse than the pain of the body.

PUBLILIUS SYRUS (CA. 42 B.C.)

They brought unto him all sick people that were
taken with diverse diseases and torments . . . and he
healed them.

MATTHEW 4:24

For our light affliction, which is but for a moment,
worketh for us a far more exceeding and eternal
weight of glory.

2 CORINTHIANS 4:17

He said unto me, My grace is sufficient for thee: for
my strength is made perfect in weakness.

2 CORINTHIANS 12:9

Is any among you afflicted? Let him pray.

JAMES 5:13

The God of all grace . . . after that ye have suffered a
while, make you perfect, stablish, strengthen, settle
you.

1 PETER 5:10

And God shall wipe away all tears from their eyes;
and there shall be no more death, neither sorrow, nor
crying, neither shall there be any more pain: for the
former things are passed away.

REVELATION 21:4

When pain is to be borne, a little courage helps more
than much knowledge, a little human sympathy
more than much courage, and the least tincture of
the love of God more than all.

C. S. LEWIS (1898–1963)

In times like these, it helps to recall that there have
always been times like these.

PAUL HARVEY (1918–   )

It takes more distress and poison to kill someone
who has peace of mind and loves life.

BERNIE S. SIEGEL, M.D. (1928–   )

Diseases can be our spiritual flat tires—disruptions
in our lives that seem to be disasters at the time but
end by redirecting our lives in a meaningful way.

BERNIE S. SIEGEL, M.D. (1928–   )

One cannot get through life without pain. . . . What
we can do is choose how to use the pain life presents
to us.

BERNIE S. SIEGEL, M.D. (1928–   )

Eleven
Healing

While I was completing this book I met a friend whose son has been plagued by severe emotional problems. "Last Sunday," my friend said, "my son asked me to go to a church that helps him feel better. As soon as I went in, I looked around with interest because there were so many young people present. Some of them were playing drums and guitars and other instruments. The music had a fast beat that I don't usually associate with church. But it was lively, and nearly everyone present was singing and either clapping or raising their hands.

"During a prayer," my friend went on, "the pastor said, 'Lord, we renounce defeat. We renounce poverty. We renounce sickness. We claim health and prosperity and victory in the name of Jesus.' Then the pastor announced some answers to prayer, and people clapped. A woman stood up and said that she wanted to thank those who had been praying about the growth on her kidney. The preceding Tuesday, she said, she had got the results of a CAT scan; the growth had disappeared.

"I guess I'm fussy," my friend concluded, "because some of that isn't my cup of tea. But I wish more churches had that kind of faith and enthusiasm and positive outlook. If they did, there would probably be a lot more people in church."

The encouraging thing is that many churches today seem to be discovering anew the power of positive faith and the reality of healing. Many sick people came to Jesus long ago, and the Gospels tell us "he healed them all." Whether through the science of medicine or the force of faith, God is still healing spirits, minds, and bodies.

I am the Lord that healeth thee.

EXODUS 15:26

I shall yet praise him, who is the health of my countenance, and my God.

PSALM 42:11

I will cure them, and will reveal unto them the abundance of peace and truth.

JEREMIAH 33:6

The first petition that we are to make to Almighty
God is for a good conscience, the next for health of
mind, and then of body.

LUCIUS ANNAEUS SENECA (4 B.C.–A.D. 65)

To wish to be well is a part of becoming well.

LUCIUS ANNAEUS SENECA (4 B.C.–A.D. 65)

Thy faith hath made thee whole.

MATTHEW 9:22

He ordained twelve . . . to have power to heal
sicknesses, and to cast out devils.

MARK 3:14–15

The power of the Lord was present to heal them.

LUKE 5:17

In that same hour he cured many of their infirmities.

LUKE 7:21

Jesus Christ maketh thee whole.

ACTS 9:34

And the leaves of the tree were for the healing of the nations.

REVELATION 22:2

Humanity . . . created sick, commanded to be sound.

SIR FULKE GREVILLE (1554—1628)

What wound did ever heal but by degrees?

WILLIAM SHAKESPEARE (1564—1616)

Sleep that knits up the ravell'd sleave of care,
The death of each day's life, sore labor's bath,
Balm of hurt minds, great nature's second course,
Chief nourisher in life's feast.

WILLIAM SHAKESPEARE (1564—1616)

He healeth those that are broken in heart: and giveth medicine to heal their sickness.

THE BOOK OF COMMON PRAYER

Health and cheerfulness mutually beget each other.

JOSEPH ADDISON (1672–1719)

How sweet the name of Jesus sounds
In a believer's ear!
It soothes his sorrows, heals his wounds,
And drives away his fear.

EDWARD PERRONET (1721–1792)

Jesus speaks, and speaks to thee . . .
I deliver'd thee when bound,
And, when bleeding, heal'd thy wound;
Sought thee wand'ring, set thee right,
Turn'd thy darkness into light.

WILLIAM COWPER (1731–1800)

Sometimes a light surprises
The Christian while he sings;
It is the Lord who rises
With healing in his wings.

WILLIAM COWPER (1731–1800)

Our Creator has given us five senses to help us
survive threats from the external world, and a sixth
sense, our healing system, to help us survive internal
threats.

BERNIE S. SIEGEL, M.D. (1928–   )

Feelings are chemical and can kill or cure.

BERNIE S. SIEGEL, M.D. (1928–   )

Twelve
Community

The ancient words, "It is not good that the man should be alone" (*Genesis 2:18*), apply to more than love and marriage. Modern science is replete with evidence that it is good for human beings to live in community, to relate constructively to others in various ways, from local groups to patriotic endeavors and worldwide ventures in brotherhood and sisterhood.

While I was an active pastor, I supported ecumenical efforts and councils of churches. At one gathering of the New York City Council of Churches, of which I was once president, I remarked that if no such organization existed, someone would have had to invent it, so important is its work. I have long been active in Rotary and similar organizations where there is not only camaraderie but participation in projects of goodwill.

And I am an enthusiastic citizen of the United States of America. This country's great heritage of freedom comes from the mingling of two mighty streams. One stream is that of classical antiquity. The great thinkers of ancient Greece held that the human mind is sacred and that no one must enslave it. The other stream is that of the Judeo-Christian heritage, which upholds the infinite worth and the right to freedom of every individual.

It is very interesting that this ideal of freedom is now being sought, and often celebrated, in almost every country on earth. For the idea of community cannot be satisfied until it embraces the whole world. The ancient prophets and mystics had a noble vision of worldwide human kinship and peace. As we reach out positively to others, each one of us can bring that vision closer to reality.

To do justice and judgment is more acceptable to the Lord than sacrifice.

PROVERBS 21:3

If thine enemy be hungry, give him bread to eat; and if he be thirsty, give him water to drink.

PROVERBS 25:21

Where there is no vision, the people perish: but he
that keepeth the law, happy is he.

PROVERBS 29:18

Learn to do well; seek judgment, relieve the
oppressed, judge the fatherless, plead for the widow.

ISAIAH 1:17

They shall beat their swords into plowshares, and
their swords into pruninghooks: nation shall not lift
up sword against nation, neither shall they learn war
any more.

ISAIAH 2:4

Oh, what times! Oh, what standards!

MARCUS TULLIUS CICERO (106–43 B.C.)

Who, then, is free? The wise man who can govern
himself.

HORACE (QUINTUS HORATIUS FLACCUS, 65–8 B.C.)

I found Rome a city of bricks, and left it a city of
marble.

AUGUSTUS CAESAR (63 B.C.–A.D. 14)

Blessed are the peacemakers.

MATTHEW 5:9

All they that take the sword shall perish with the
sword.

MATTHEW 26:52

Pure religion and undefiled before God and the
Father is this, to visit the fatherless and widows in
their affliction, and to keep himself unspotted from
the world.

JAMES 1:27

Play the man, Master Ridley; we shall this day light
such a candle, by God's grace, in England, as I trust
shall never be put out.

HUGH LATIMER (1485–1555)

Heaven is above all yet; there sits a judge
That no king can corrupt.

WILLIAM SHAKESPEARE (1564–1616)

Nothing emboldens sin so much as mercy.

WILLIAM SHAKESPEARE (1564–1616)

I pray heaven to bestow the best of all blessings on this house and all that hereafter shall inhabit it. May none but honest and wise men ever rule under this roof.

JOHN ADAMS (1725–1826), INSCRIPTION IN WHITE HOUSE

Rebellion to tyrants is obedience to God.

THOMAS JEFFERSON (1743–1826)

The God who gave us life gave us liberty at the same time.

THOMAS JEFFERSON (1743–1826)

Man's inhumanity to man makes countless thousands mourn.

ROBERT BURNS (1759–1796)

Whither is fled the visionary gleam
Where is it now, the glory and the dream?

WILLIAM WORDSWORTH (1770–1850)

113

Breathes there the man, with soul so dead,
Who never to himself hath said,
This is my own, my native land!

SIR WALTER SCOTT (1771–1832)

Greater than the tread of mighty armies is an idea
whose time has come.

VICTOR HUGO (1802–1885)

This will remain the land of the free only so long as
it is the land of the brave.

ELMER DAVIS (1890–1958)

Either war is obsolete or men are.

R. BUCKMINSTER FULLER (1895–1983)

I decline to accept the end of man.

WILLIAM FAULKNER (1897–1962)

Those who corrupt the public mind are just as evil as
those who steal from the public purse.

ADLAI STEVENSON (1900–1965)

Learning isn't a means to an end; it is an end in itself.

ROBERT A. HEINLEIN (1907–   )

Unfortunately, many Americans live on the outskirts of hope—some because of their poverty, some because of their color, and all too many because of both. Our task is to help replace their despair with opportunity.

LYNDON BAINES JOHNSON (1908–1973)

We are confronted primarily with a moral issue. It is as old as the Scriptures and is as clear as the American Constitution.

JOHN F. KENNEDY (1917–1963)

Education's purpose is to replace an empty mind with an open one.

MALCOLM S. FORBES (1919–1990)

Injustice anywhere is a threat to justice everywhere.

MARTIN LUTHER KING, JR. (1929–1968)

■

We shall overcome, we shall overcome
We shall overcome someday
Oh, deep in my heart, I do believe
We shall overcome someday.

CIVIL RIGHTS SONG

Thirteen
Love and Family

F amily trees are interesting. My mother's father, Andrew DeLaney, was born in Ballynakill, Ireland. But as a lad he stowed away on a ship bound for America, where he married blue-eyed Margaret Potts and became an industrious Ohioan. My mother, Anna DeLaney, had a face matched by the beauty of her character. A hard worker, she took a happy delight in life and possessed the gift of infectious laughter.

The Peales came from England; my great grandfather Thomas Peale was one of the early settlers of Lynchburg, Ohio. His sons Samuel and Wilson Peale operated a dry-goods store. My father, Charles Clifford Peale, was trained as a physician and, after practicing medicine for some time, became a full-time minister. As both an M.D. and a D.D., Father sometimes punned whimsically that he was a "pair-o'-docs." Father was one of the first men to demonstrate the partnership of spiritual with physical health.

My wife Ruth's parents were Canadians. Her father, Frank Burton Stafford, was a minister, one of the finest men I have ever known. Her mother, Loretta Crosby Stafford, combined a saintly character with strength and firmness.

The dynamic qualities of enthusiasm, excitement, energy, and faith run like golden cords through the lives of the Staffords, the Peales, the Crosbys, and the DeLaneys. And they manifest themselves in each of our children—Margaret, John, and Elizabeth—and their spouses and children. How fortunate I am to be part of such a splendid family.

Families, like individuals, are unique. Cherish your family connections. They are one of God's greatest ways of demonstrating his love and fellowship.

A friend loveth at all times, and a brother is born for adversity.

PROVERBS 17:17

His banner over me was love.

SONG OF SOLOMON 2:4

Many waters cannot quench love, neither can the
floods drown it.

SONG OF SOLOMON 8:7

One's best asset is a sympathetic spouse.

EURIPIDES (485–406 B.C.)

Absence makes the heart grow fonder.

SEXTUS AURELIUS PROPERTIUS (54 B.C.–A.D. 2)

Love yields to business. If you seek a way out of
love, be busy; you'll be safe then.

OVID (43 B.C.–A.D. 18)

By this shall all men know that ye are my disciples,
if ye have love one to another.

JOHN 13:35

Love worketh no ill to his neighbor: therefore love is
the fulfilling of the law.

ROMANS 13:10

The fruit of the Spirit is love.

GALATIANS 5:22

If any provide not for his own, and specially for those
of his own house, he hath denied the faith, and is
worse than an infidel.

1 TIMOTHY 5:8

Beloved, let us love one another: for love is of God;
and every one that loveth is born of God.

1 JOHN 4:7

Who has never tasted what is bitter does not know
what is sweet.

GERMAN PROVERB

I speak Spanish to God, Italian to women, French to
men, and German to my horse.

CHARLES V OF FRANCE (1337–1380)

There is no more lovely, friendly, and charming
relationship, communion, or company than a good
marriage.

MARTIN LUTHER (1483–1546)

The heart has reasons which the reason cannot understand.

BLAISE PASCAL (1623–1662)

There are three faithful friends—an old wife, an old dog, and ready money.

BENJAMIN FRANKLIN (1706–1790)

Mid pleasures and palaces though we may roam,
Be it ever so humble, there's no place like home.

JOHN HOWARD PAYNE (1791–1852)

'Tis better to have loved and lost
Than never to have loved at all.

ALFRED LORD TENNYSON (1809–1892)

Love is a gentle courtesy.

ANONYMOUS

Her voice is full of money.

ANONYMOUS

It is better not to live than not to love.

HENRY DRUMMOND (1851–1897)

Holy Matrimony; which is an honorable estate,
instituted of God in the time of innocency, signifying
unto us the mystical union that is betwixt Christ
and his Church.

THE BOOK OF COMMON PRAYER

The holy estate of matrimony . . . to have and to
hold from this day forward, for better for worse, for
richer for poorer, in sickness and in health, to love
and to cherish, till death do us part.

THE BOOK OF COMMON PRAYER

Fourteen
Aging

The process of aging is often thought of as a slow, sad descent into the grave. I suppose I am fortunate in having been exposed all my life to dynamic men and women who lived to a vigorous old age and whose passing from this life seemed not a defeat but a celebration. My parents, my wife's parents, and many of our ancestors lived considerably beyond the traditional "threescore years and ten." And I have often been impressed by people who displayed uncommon energy and good health into their seventies, eighties, and nineties.

One such person was William H. Danforth, head of the Ralston Purina Company, who, as a sickly child, accepted his teacher's dare to become the healthiest boy in his class. He not only did so but inspired thousands of others to be their best both physically and spiritually with his book *I Dare You*. In his "old age," Danforth was an amazing example of tireless energy. So was the vaudeville entertainer Mort Cheshire, who still played the "bones" vigorously at the age of one hundred and two.

Nearly forty years ago, I wrote in *The Power of Positive Thinking*, "The longer I live the more I am convinced that neither age nor circumstance need to deprive us of energy and vitality." I still find that true. Although I have retired from my church, I occupy my working hours with *Guideposts* magazine, the Foundation for Christian Living, speaking, and writing books and articles. I go to bed as early as possible every night, usually sleep soundly and rise early. I try to eat sensibly, exercise regularly, and avoid bad habits of all kinds.

I mentally repudiate physical, mental, or spiritual decline or disability. I trust in the living God. And I recommend the same to anyone who desires a long and healthy life.

And Moses was a hundred and twenty years old
when he died: his eye was not dim, nor his natural
force abated.

DEUTERONOMY 34:7

The Lord blessed the latter end of Job more than the
beginning.

JOB 42:12

124

So teach us to number our days, that we may apply
our hearts unto wisdom.

PSALM 90:12

They shall still bring forth fruit in old age.

PSALM 92:14

The hoary head is a crown of glory.

PROVERBS 16:31

Your old men shall dream dreams.

JOEL 2:28

It is always in season for old men to learn.

AESCHYLUS (525–456 B. C.)

He who is of a calm and happy nature will hardly
feel the pressure of age.

PLATO (427–347 B.C.)

Give me a young man in whom there is something
of the old, and an old man in whom there is
something of the young. Guided so, a man may grow
old in body but never in mind.

MARCUS TULLIUS CICERO (106–43 B.C.)

Perhaps someday it will be pleasant to remember
even this.

VIRGIL (PUBLIUS VERGILIUS MARO, 70–19 B.C.)

The years as they pass plunder us of one thing after
another.

HORACE (QUINTUS HORATIUS FLACCUS, 65–8 B.C.)

A man's life is what his thoughts make of it.

MARCUS AURELIUS (121–180)

All is well that ends well.

JOHN HEYWOOD (1497–1580)

The proof of the pudding is in the eating.

MIGUEL DE CERVANTES (1546–1611)

Man wants but little here below, nor wants that
little long.

OLIVER GOLDSMITH (1728–1774)

We grow gray in our spirit long before we grow gray
in our hair.

CHARLES LAMB (1775–1834)

When I go down to the grave I can say I have
finished my day's work. But I cannot say I have
finished my life. My day's work will begin again the
next morning.

VICTOR HUGO (1802–1885)

We do not count a man's years until he has nothing
else to count.

RALPH WALDO EMERSON (1803–1882)

For of all sad words of tongues or pen
The saddest are these: It might have been.

JOHN GREENLEAF WHITTIER (1807–1892)

∎

Time's wheel runs back or stops: Potter and clay
endure.

ROBERT BROWNING (1812–1889)

∎

None are so old as those who have outlived
enthusiasm.

HENRY DAVID THOREAU (1817–1862)

∎

To know how to grow old is the master-work of
wisdom, and one of the most difficult chapters in the
great art of living.

HENRI FREDERIC AMIEL (1821–1881)

∎

If wrinkles must be written upon our brows, let
them not be written upon the heart. The spirit
should not grow old.

JAMES A. GARFIELD (1831–1881)

When life was like a story, holding neither sob nor sigh
In the golden olden glory of the days gone by.

JAMES WHITCOMB RILEY (1849–1916)

Little by little the time goes by,
Short if you sing it, long if you sigh.

ANONYMOUS

We may let go all things which we cannot carry into
the eternal life.

ANNA R. BROWN LINDSAY (1864–1948)

I dare you to be healthy, live a long time, and never
think old age.

WILLIAM H. DANFORTH (1870–1955)

It is wonderful to be young, but it is equally
desirable to be mature and rich in experience.

BERNARD BARUCH (1870–1965)

I am not interested in the past. I am interested in the
future, for that is where I expect to spend the rest of
my life.

CHARLES F. KETTERING (1876–1958)

Live your life and forget your age.

FRANK BERING (1877–1965)

■

If you wait for the perfect moment when all is safe
and assured, it may never arrive. Mountains will not
be climbed, races won, or lasting happiness achieved.

MAURICE CHEVALIER (1888–1972)

■

Never think any oldish thoughts. It's oldish thoughts
that make a person old.

JAMES A. FARLEY (1888–1976)

■

Every business organization should have a
vice-president in charge of constant renewal.

DWAYNE ORTON (1903–1971)

■

Don't look back. Something may be gaining on you.

SATCHEL PAIGE (1906–1982)

■

If you carry your childhood with you, you never
become older.

ABRAHAM SUTZKEVER (1913–   )

To those who shall sit here rejoicing, and to those
who shall sit here lamenting—greeting and
sympathy. So have we done in our time.

BENCH INSCRIPTION, CORNELL UNIVERSITY

The future is something which everyone reaches at
the rate of sixty minutes an hour, whatever he does,
whoever he is.

C. S. LEWIS (1898–1963)

Fifteen
Death and Beyond

———————■———————

What we call death comes eventually to every one of us. And the loss of a loved one is usually a heartrending experience.

Early in my ministry, I noticed a black wreath on a door in my city parish. It was the Christmas season. I did not know anyone at the address, but I knocked on the door and discovered that a little girl had died. When I saw that beautiful child in her casket, I wanted to hold the parents in my arms and weep with them. I could hardly find words to express my feelings. But the bereaved father and mother must have felt my grief, for what I did say seemed to give them some comfort.

One of my lifelong convictions is that death, far from being the end, is but the door to an existence larger and more glorious than any human conception. Years ago, my wife, Ruth, and I took a helicopter ride above the Swiss Alps. Leaving the heliport at Zermatt, we flew up a green valley and doubled back over the little toy village far below. Then we soared past the peaks of Gornergrat and Stockhorn and over a vast gleaming glacier.

But suddenly the glacier came to an abrupt end. We hung suspended over what seemed to be *nothing*. We were at least eleven thousand feet high—and it seemed as though there was only an empty void below. Later Ruth wrote about that flight, "Perhaps dying is like that: an outward rush into the unknown where there is nothing recognizable, nothing to cling to, and yet you are sustained and supported over the great void just as you were over the comfortable and familiar terrain."

Helen Steiner Rice once wrote, "The end of the road is but a bend in the road." I believe that is true of life and death. At the end of God's world there is his endless world beyond.

Naked came I out of my mother's womb, and naked shall I return thither: the Lord gave, and the Lord hath taken away; blessed be the name of the Lord.

JOB 1:21

I know that my Redeemer liveth.

JOB 19:25

Though I walk through the valley of the shadow of
death, I will fear no evil: for thou art with me.

PSALM 23:4

Pale death with impartial tread beats at the poor
man's cottage door and at the palaces of kings.

HORACE (QUINTUS HORATIUS FLACCUS, 65–8 B.C.)

Peace I leave with you, my peace I give unto you:
not as the world giveth, give I unto you.

JOHN 14:27

Our Saviour Jesus Christ, who hath abolished death,
and hath brought life and immortality to light
through the gospel.

2 TIMOTHY 1:10

Blessed are the dead who die in the Lord from
henceforth: Yea, saith the Spirit, that they may rest
from their labors.

REVELATION 14:13

There shall be no more death.

REVELATION 21:4

As a well-spent day brings happy sleep, so life well
used brings happy death.

LEONARDO DA VINCI (1452–1519)

■

To be or not to be, that is the question.

WILLIAM SHAKESPEARE (1564–1616)

■

No man is an island, entire of itself; every man is a
piece of the continent, a part of the main. If a clod be
washed away by the sea, Europe is the less, as well
as if a promontory were, as well as if a manor of thy
friend's or of thine own were. Any man's death
diminishes me because I am involved in mankind;
and therefore never send to know for whom the bell
tolls; it tolls for thee.

JOHN DONNE (1572–1631)

■

It is so soon that I am done for
I wonder what I was begun for.

TOMBSTONE INSCRIPTION, CHELTENHAM

■

Hide me, O my Savior, hide,
Till the storm of life be past;

Safe into the haven guide,
O receive my soul at last.

CHARLES WESLEY (1707–1788)

It is well. I die hard but I am not afraid to go.

GEORGE WASHINGTON (1732–1799)

We do not believe in immortality because we can
prove it, but we try to prove it because we cannot
help believing it.

HARRIET MARTINEAU (1802–1876)

Now I lay me down to sleep.
I pray thee, Lord, my soul to keep.
If I should die before I wake,
I pray thee, Lord, my soul to take
And this I ask for Jesus' sake.

ANONYMOUS

I know not where his islands lift
Their fronded palms in air;
I only know I cannot drift
Beyond his love and care.

JOHN GREENLEAF WHITTIER (1807–1892)

137

Yet Love will dream, and Faith will trust
(Since he knows our need is just),
That somehow, somewhere, meet we must.
—Life is ever lord of Death
And Love can never lose its own.

JOHN GREENLEAF WHITTIER (1807–1892)

O Christ, that it were possible
For one short hour to see
The souls we loved, that they may tell us
What and where they be.

ALFRED LORD TENNYSON (1809–1892)

Thou wilt not leave us in the dust.
Thou madest man, he knows not why;
He thinks he was not made to die.
Thou hast made him; thou art just.

ALFRED LORD TENNYSON (1809–1892)

We are citizens of eternity.

FEODOR DOSTOEVSKI (1821–1881)

138

In the night of death hope sees a star and listening
love can hear the rustle of a wing.

ROBERT INGERSOLL (1833–1899)

When a man dies, if he can pass enthusiasm along to
his children, he has left them an estate of
incalculable value.

THOMAS A. EDISON (1847–1931)

Think of him still as the same, I say,
He is not dead; he is just—away.

JAMES WHITCOMB RILEY (1849–1916)

When the one Great Scorer comes to write against
your name, he marks not that you won or lost, but
how you played the game.

GRANTLAND RICE (1880–1954)

Who may regret what was, since it has made Himself
himself?

JOHN FREEMAN (1881–1929)

In the heart of London City,
'Mid the dwellings of the poor,
These bright, golden words were uttered,
"I have Christ! What want I more?"
Spoken by a lonely woman,
Dying on a garret floor,
Having not one earthly comfort—
"I have Christ! What want I more?"

ANONYMOUS

For Jack and Marsha Countryman.
God thinks you're wonderful, and so do I.
MAX LUCADO

To my dad, Bill Givens,
with "such happiness."
CHRIS SHEA